# HOLD ON

Staying Present When Everything Moves

By: Trent Goodbaudy

Copyright © 2026 Trent Goodbaudy
All rights reserved.
ISBN: 9798243326490

# DEDICATION

**For my daughter.**

Trent Goodbaudy

# Table of Contents

Opening — Before the Waves .................................................................3
PART I — WHEN THE WATER MOVES ......................................7
   Chapter 1 — The First Tilt...................................................................8
   Chapter 2 — Why Your Nervous System Feels It First .............15
   Chapter 3 — When Meaning Slips ..................................................21
   Chapter 4 — The Illusion of Stability.............................................27
PART II — WHEN NOTHING COMES BACK......................31
   Chapter 5 — The Silence After You Speak....................................33
   Chapter 6 — Dismissal, Mockery, and the Laughing Emoji ........39
   Chapter 7 — Being Seen and Not Met ............................................45
   Chapter 8 — Why Sincerity Feels Dangerous to Others ..............49
PART III — WHEN YOU STAY ......................................................53
   Chapter 9 — What It Means to Remain..........................................55
   Chapter 10 — Holding Without Hardening...................................59
   Chapter 11 — The Quiet Strength Nobody Applauds ..................63
   Chapter 12 — Staying When Everything Moves..........................67
Closing — You're Still Here ................................................................71
About the Author ...................................................................................75
About LibertyTruth ................................................................................77

Trent Goodbaudy

# ACKNOWLEDGMENTS

To those who stayed present when nothing was certain.
To the moments of silence that made listening possible.
And to the unseen patience that carried this book into being.

Thank you.

**EYE OF THE STORM**

You don't have to understand what's happening.
You don't have to decide what it means.
You don't have to know where this goes.

Everything is moving.
That doesn't mean you are lost.

The waves can be loud.
The sky can look broken.
The world can feel like it is rearranging itself without asking.

And still —
you are here.

Breathing.
Sensing.
Touching something real.

This is not the calm after the storm.
This is the stillness *inside* it.

Nothing needs to be fixed in this moment.
Nothing needs to be proven.

Just stay.

You are not behind.
You are not wrong.
You are not failing.

You are weathering.

Trent Goodbaudy

## Opening — Before the Waves

There are moments when nothing is wrong, and yet everything feels unsteady.

Not because something has broken.
Not because a crisis has arrived.
But because something underneath your life has shifted, and your body knows it before your thoughts do.

You might notice it in small ways.
A pause where there used to be certainty.
A hesitation where there used to be momentum.
A quiet, almost imperceptible sense that the ground you've been standing on isn't quite where it was yesterday.

Most people rush past that feeling.
They distract themselves, explain it away, or try to cover it with activity. They call it anxiety, boredom, burnout, or mood. They give it a name so they don't have to listen to it.

But what you're feeling in those moments is not a problem.
It's a **movement**.

And movement, even when it's natural, can feel like danger.

This book exists for the space between those two things.

Not to stop the movement.
Not to make it go away.
But to help you stay present inside it.

You don't need to be fearless to read this book.
You don't need to be healed, confident, or certain.

You only need to be here.

Because what most people discover, sooner or later, is that life does not become stable before it becomes meaningful. It becomes meaningful *inside* instability — inside change, inside loss, inside the quiet moments when nothing is returning the signals you're sending out.

There is a particular kind of loneliness that appears when you put something real into the world.

It might be a book.
A relationship.
A truth.
A version of yourself that is more honest than what you've shown before.

You offer it.
And then… nothing.

No echo.
No reflection.
No clear sign that it was received.

That silence can feel heavier than rejection.
At least rejection has shape.

Silence just sits there, and you start filling it with questions.

Was it a mistake?
Was I foolish to care?
Did I misread something?

Those questions are not weakness.
They are the natural response of a nervous system that reached out and didn't feel a hand come back.

This book is not here to answer those questions with advice or slogans.

It's here to do something simpler and much harder.

It's here to keep you company while they exist.

You are not meant to be a statue in a storm.
You are meant to be a person in it.

That means sometimes you will sway.
Sometimes you will doubt.
Sometimes you will feel small in a very large, very moving world.

None of that means you are failing.

It means you are still in contact.

**Hold On** is not a command.
It's a description.

It's what happens when you stay present even when certainty leaves.
When you don't harden.
When you don't disappear.
When you don't turn yourself into a performance to be rewarded.

You don't have to understand everything that moves through you as you read this.
You don't have to agree with everything.

All that's asked of you here is what's asked of you in a storm:

Stay.

The waves will do what they do.
The sky will move how it moves.

You don't need to master any of it.

You just need to still be here when the next page turns.

Trent Goodbaudy

# PART I — WHEN THE WATER MOVES

## Chapter 1 — The First Tilt

**The moment something you trusted starts to shift**

It rarely announces itself.

There is no alarm when the thing you've been standing on begins to move. No clear sound that tells you, *This is the moment everything changed.* Most of the time, it feels so small you almost miss it.

A comment that lands differently than you expected.
A silence where there used to be warmth.
A result that doesn't match the effort you gave.

You tell yourself it's nothing.
You keep going.

But something inside you has already noticed.

The first tilt isn't dramatic. It's subtle. It's the sensation of being just a fraction of a degree off from where you were a moment ago.
You're still upright. You're still functioning. You're still doing what you do.

And yet…
something doesn't quite line up anymore.

We're taught to trust stories more than sensations.
If nothing visibly broke, we assume nothing changed. But your

nervous system doesn't work that way. It tracks shifts in connection, safety, and meaning long before your mind can make sense of them.

That's why you can feel unsettled even when everything looks fine.

You might still be in the same job.
Still in the same relationship.
Still walking through the same days.

But the *feeling* of standing there has altered.

That's the first tilt.

It happens when something you relied on — a person, a belief, a role, a sense of being understood — moves just enough that your inner balance has to adjust. You don't fall. You just… compensate.

You lean a little.
You hold a little tighter.
You think a little harder.

And for a while, that works.

This is why so many people don't realize they're in a storm until they're already deep inside it. They've been quietly shifting their weight for so long that they think the strain they feel is just life.

But it isn't.

It's adaptation.

When something you trusted begins to change, your body responds before your thoughts do. Your breathing gets shallower. Your attention sharpens. Your emotional range narrows. You start scanning for what might go wrong, even if you can't say why.

None of that means you're broken.

It means you're still connected.

Disconnection is numb.
Presence is sensitive.

So when you feel that first, barely noticeable instability — the sense that the ground is no longer where it was — that is not weakness.

It is the most honest part of you saying, *Something has moved.*

The problem is not that things shift.

The problem is what we do when they do.

Most of us were taught that stability is something you achieve and then protect. So when it wobbles, we panic. We grasp. We try to force things back into the shape they used to be.

But the first tilt is not asking you to fix anything.

It's asking you to notice.

Because before there are waves, before there is chaos, before there is anything dramatic at all, there is just this:

A quiet change in how it feels to be here.

And that is where **Hold On** begins.

## How Your Body Notices Before Your Mind Does

Your body is not philosophical.

It doesn't argue.
It doesn't explain.
It doesn't justify.

It simply responds.

That's why it is always the first thing to know when something has shifted. Long before you can name what's wrong, your body has already begun to change how it holds itself in the world.

Your shoulders lift.
Your jaw tightens.
Your breathing gets smaller.
Your attention sharpens in a way that feels like alertness but is really anticipation.

You may not even notice it happening. Most of us were trained out of feeling these micro-adjustments. We were taught to listen to stories instead — to reasons, explanations, narratives about why everything is fine.

But your nervous system doesn't speak in sentences.

It speaks in sensation.

It registers when connection feels thinner.
When safety feels less reliable.
When meaning feels less anchored.

And it does this without asking permission from your mind.

That's why the first sign of a storm is often something vague: a restlessness, a heaviness, a sense of being slightly "off." You can't point to anything concrete, so you assume it must be you.

But what you're feeling is not a flaw.
It's a signal.

Your body is designed to detect movement in the environment — not just physical movement, but relational, emotional, and psychological movement too. When the ground beneath you changes, even subtly, your body shifts to keep you upright.

That's what anxiety really is at its core:
a body preparing for change before the mind knows what to do with it.

So when something you trust starts to move — a relationship, a project, a sense of being seen — your body leans forward, scanning for what might come next. It's trying to keep you in contact with what's real.

The tragedy is that we often mistake this intelligence for dysfunction.

We tell ourselves to calm down.
We distract ourselves.
We override what we feel with what we think should be true.

And in doing so, we disconnect from the very system that is trying to keep us present.

This book is not about learning to ignore those signals.

It's about learning to stay with them without being consumed.

Your body noticing first is not a problem to solve.

It's the beginning of holding on.

Because when everything moves, the only thing that can keep you here is contact — with your breath, your sensations, your aliveness.

Before there is any story about what is happening, there is just this:

You are here.
Something has shifted.
And you are still breathing.

That is not fear.

That is awareness.

## EYE OF THE STORM

You don't have to make sense of what you just felt.

You don't have to decide if it was real.
You don't have to label it.

Something moved.
You noticed.

That's enough for now.

Your body is already doing what it knows how to do — adjusting, breathing, staying upright inside change. You don't have to help it by rushing, fixing, or explaining.

Let the waves roll.
Let the thoughts come and go.

You are still here.

The storm is not something you have to defeat.
It is something you are already inside.

And in this moment —
you are holding.

# Chapter 2 — Why Your Nervous System Feels It First

**The Difference Between Danger and Motion**

Your nervous system is designed to keep you alive, not to make you comfortable.

It doesn't ask, *Is this good or bad?*
It asks, *Is this changing?*

That's an important distinction — and it's one most of us were never taught.

When something in your life begins to move — a relationship shifts, a sense of belonging thins, a project stops feeling held — your body reacts as if something might be wrong, even if nothing is technically broken.

Because from a biological perspective, **change itself is a risk**.

For most of human history, stability meant survival. Predictable food, predictable shelter, predictable people. Sudden shifts in the environment were often followed by real danger. So the nervous system learned a simple rule:

Movement = Pay attention.

But in modern life, movement happens constantly. Social structures change. Digital spaces fluctuate. Relationships stretch and shrink. Meaning comes and goes. Your body is still using an ancient operating system to interpret all of it.

So when something moves emotionally or relationally, your nervous system doesn't calmly file it under "growth." It flags it as potential threat.

That's why you can feel anxious in situations that aren't actually dangerous.

You're not afraid of harm.
You're feeling **motion**.

The trouble starts when we confuse the two.

When your body senses motion, it activates — heart rate up, muscles tight, attention narrowed. That feels like fear. So the mind steps in and tries to find something to be afraid of. It builds a story to match the sensation.

Maybe I did something wrong.
Maybe they're pulling away.
Maybe this is falling apart.

But the sensation came first.
The story came later.

This is why so many emotional storms feel bigger than the events that triggered them. The nervous system is responding to instability, not to a specific outcome.

You are not weak for feeling unsettled when things shift.

You are sensitive to movement.

And sensitivity, in this context, is not fragility. It is contact with reality.

The storm begins not when something goes wrong, but when something starts to move.

The practice of holding on begins right there — not by forcing things to stop, but by staying present while they do.

## Why Uncertainty Feels Like a Threat

Your nervous system does not experience uncertainty as neutral.

It experiences it as **exposure**.

When you don't know what will happen next, your body can't predict how to keep you safe. That lack of prediction is what creates the feeling of threat — not because something bad is happening, but because something *unknown* might.

To a nervous system, not knowing is worse than knowing something painful.

At least pain has shape.
At least danger has edges.

Uncertainty has none.

So when a relationship becomes ambiguous, when a future stops looking clear, when something you were counting on no longer feels reliable, your body tightens. Your breathing changes. Your attention scans the horizon.

You feel restless.
Or numb.
Or suddenly very tired.

These are not failures of will.

They are survival responses.

Your nervous system is trying to find ground where there is none. It is searching for something stable to stand on so it can relax again.

This is why people often cling to stories when they're uncertain — even painful stories.

"I know this is bad, but at least I know what it is."
"I know they don't care, but at least that makes sense."
"I know I failed, but at least that explains the feeling."

The mind prefers a bad conclusion to no conclusion at all.

But the truth is that uncertainty is not an enemy.

It is a moment when reality is still forming.

The problem is that your nervous system wants closure before life has provided it. It wants a map before the landscape has finished shifting.

So it presses you to resolve things prematurely: to assume, to decide, to lock into an interpretation that brings the sensation of not-knowing to an end.

That relief is tempting.

But it often costs you something more valuable: contact with what is actually happening.

To hold on in uncertainty does not mean you feel calm.

It means you stay.

You stay with the breath that doesn't know yet.
You stay with the sensations that are still moving.
You stay with the moment before meaning hardens into story.

That is not passivity.

That is presence.

And presence is what allows you to remain real while the world rearranges itself around you.

## EYE OF THE STORM

You don't have to resolve what you don't yet understand.

You don't have to force the fog to lift.
You don't have to decide what this means.

Something is still moving.
That's not a mistake.

Your breath is here.
Your body is here.
Your attention is here.

That's ground enough.

Uncertainty is not a hole you are falling into.
It is a space you are standing inside.

You are allowed to stand here
without answers,
without conclusions,
without fear deciding for you.

Hold.

Trent Goodbaudy

# Chapter 3 — When Meaning Slips

## Losing Traction with Something You Cared About

There is a particular kind of pain that doesn't come from being hurt, but from being **unheld**.

Not attacked.
Not betrayed.
Just... no longer carried by the thing that used to support you.

You might still be doing the same work.
Still showing up.
Still offering the same care, the same attention, the same effort.

But the feeling of being met has thinned.

It's like walking on a surface that used to grip your feet and suddenly doesn't. You don't fall right away. You slide. You overcorrect. You tense up in small, invisible ways trying to keep your balance.

That's what it feels like when meaning begins to slip.

What makes this so disorienting is that nothing obvious has to go wrong. There's no single moment you can point to and say, *That's when it broke.* Instead, there's a slow erosion of resonance. The thing you cared about no longer answers you in the same way.

You speak, and the echo is faint.
You give, and it doesn't quite land.
You show up, and it doesn't feel like anyone is really there.

This kind of loss is easy to dismiss because it doesn't look like loss. But inside, something very real is happening: your sense of **connection to what you're doing** is weakening.

We are not sustained by effort alone.
We are sustained by **feedback** — not applause, but contact.

When you care about something, you are in relationship with it. You feel when it responds. You feel when it doesn't. And when that response fades, your whole system starts to wonder what it's standing on.

That's why losing traction with something you loved can feel more painful than outright rejection. Rejection has clarity. Slippage has ambiguity.

You start asking quiet questions:

Am I still needed here?
Does this still matter?
Did something change — or did I?

Those questions don't come from insecurity.
They come from **attunement**.

You are sensing that the bond between you and what you cared about is no longer what it was. That doesn't mean you did anything wrong. It means the relational field has shifted.

And when meaning slips, the world can suddenly feel very wide and very thin.

Not empty — just unsupported.

That's the moment when holding on becomes something more than a phrase.

It becomes the act of staying present even when the ground doesn't quite catch you anymore.

## The Quiet Grief of Something Not Holding

There is a kind of grief that doesn't look like grief.

It doesn't come with tears, or goodbyes, or a clear ending. It comes with a dull, persistent ache — the feeling that something you were leaning on is no longer there in the same way.

Nothing dramatic happened.
No door slammed.
No one said, "This is over."

And yet...
you feel less supported than you did before.

That's because grief doesn't only come from loss.

It also comes from **slippage**.

When something that used to hold your weight begins to soften, your whole system notices. You start carrying more of yourself than you used to. You don't even realize you're doing it at first. You just feel more tired. More strained. Less sure.

You may start to blame yourself.

Maybe I'm asking too much.
Maybe I changed.
Maybe I should try harder.

But the grief you're feeling is not about effort.

It's about **contact**.

You were in relationship with something — a person, a purpose, a dream, a sense of being seen — and that relationship is no longer giving back in the same way. The bond has loosened.

That loosening hurts even if nothing else is wrong.

Because to be held is not just to be supported.
It is to be recognized.

When something stops holding you, you don't just lose stability. You lose a part of the reflection that told you who you were.

That's why this kind of grief feels so quiet and so heavy at the same time. You can't point to it. You can't explain it to others. You just feel slightly more alone in the same place you used to feel connected.

And that loneliness is real.

You don't need to dramatize it.
You don't need to minimize it.

You just need to acknowledge what your body already knows:

Something you trusted is no longer holding you the way it once did.

That is a loss.

And it deserves to be felt — gently, honestly, without being turned into a story about failure.

This is where **Hold On** becomes more than a phrase.

Not because the grief goes away,
but because you stay present while it moves through you.

That's how something new eventually finds you.

**EYE OF THE STORM**

You don't have to rush past what you just felt.

You don't have to turn it into a problem or a plan.

Something softened.
Something loosened.
And you noticed.

That noticing is not weakness.
It is connection.

Grief does not mean you are losing yourself.
It means you are still attached to what mattered.

You are allowed to feel that.
You are allowed to pause inside it.

The storm can move through
without carrying you away.

Stay.

## Chapter 4 — The Illusion of Stability

**Why We Mistake Stillness for Safety**

We are taught, in ways so subtle we barely notice, that stability is the goal.

A steady job.
A steady relationship.
A steady identity.
A life that looks the same from one day to the next.

Stillness becomes synonymous with safety, not because it actually protects us, but because it feels predictable. And predictability gives the nervous system something it craves: the ability to relax its vigilance.

When nothing changes, your body doesn't have to scan the horizon. It can lower its guard. It can breathe.

So we start to believe that what makes us feel calm must also be what keeps us safe.

But those two things are not the same.

Stillness can be comfortable while being deeply unstable. A relationship can look peaceful while being emotionally hollow. A routine can feel secure while slowly draining your sense of meaning. A role can stay the same while no longer fitting who you are.

We don't notice this at first because nothing is overtly wrong. Everything is quiet. Everything is familiar. But inside, something begins to thin.

That thinning is what you felt in the earlier chapters — the subtle loss of traction, the quiet grief of something not holding. It happens inside stillness just as easily as it happens inside chaos.

The illusion of stability is powerful because it gives you the feeling of ground without the substance of it. You feel settled, even when what you're standing on is no longer alive.

And because we're taught to value calm above contact, we often choose that illusion over the discomfort of noticing change.

We tell ourselves:

At least nothing is blowing up.
At least it's not getting worse.
At least it's stable.

But stability that no longer holds meaning is not safety.

It's suspension.

It's the pause before something shifts.

The storm doesn't begin when things get loud.

It begins when things stop being real and start being merely still.

And learning to hold on starts with learning to tell the difference.

## What Actually Keeps You Intact

What keeps you intact is not stillness.

It is **contact**.

Contact with your body.
Contact with what you feel.
Contact with what is actually happening, rather than what you wish were happening.

Stillness can disappear in an instant.
Contact moves with you.

That's why people who build their sense of safety on external arrangements — roles, relationships, routines, identities — feel like they are falling apart when those things shift. They were standing on something that wasn't inside them.

To be intact does not mean you are unchanging.

It means you remain connected to yourself while change happens.

This is a subtle but profound difference. When you have contact, you don't need the world to stay the same for you to stay present. You can feel the ground moving and still know where you are.

You are breathing.
You are sensing.
You are aware.

Those are not abstractions. They are the raw materials of being here.

When something meaningful starts to slip, your first instinct is often to cling to the form it used to have. To try to restore the old shape, the old dynamic, the old certainty. But that usually increases the pain, because it pulls you out of contact with what is real now.

What actually keeps you intact is the ability to stay with what's happening, even when it's not what you hoped for.

That doesn't mean you like it.
It doesn't mean you approve of it.
It means you are still here inside it.

That is what holding on looks like in practice.

Not gripping the past.
Not bracing against the future.

Just staying in contact with this breath, this body, this moment — even while everything else moves.

That is the quiet, unglamorous strength this book is about.

And it is already yours.

## PART II — WHEN NOTHING COMES BACK

Trent Goodbaudy

## Chapter 5 — The Silence After You Speak

**What It Feels Like to Offer Something Real**

There is a moment when you put something honest into the world and you can feel it leave you.

It might be a truth you finally said out loud.
A piece of work you released.
A feeling you admitted.
A version of yourself you stopped hiding.

You don't always know what you're offering when you do it. You just know that something real moved through you and crossed a line from inside to outside.

That moment is strangely quiet.

Before anyone responds.
Before anything happens.

You're still there, breathing, feeling the after-echo of what you just shared.

This is where most of the vulnerability lives — not in the speaking, but in the waiting.

Your nervous system is exposed. You've opened a door. You've let something meaningful be seen. And now you're suspended between what you gave and whatever might come back.

It can feel like standing in open water.

No solid ground.
No immediate feedback.
Just you and the possibility of being met — or not.

This is not the kind of vulnerability that looks dramatic. It's not crying on the floor or making a scene. It's the soft, almost invisible courage of letting something authentic exist where others can touch it.

And because it's so quiet, it's easy to underestimate how intense it is.

You might feel a sudden urge to explain what you meant.
To soften it.
To make it safer.
To perform it in a way that will be easier to receive.

That urge isn't weakness.
It's your nervous system trying to close the door you just opened.

Because openness without response feels dangerous to a body that evolved in tribes, not on platforms or in emotionally distant rooms.

When you offer something real, you are not just sharing content.

You are extending connection.

And waiting to see if it is taken.

That waiting is where **Hold On** becomes real.

## Why the World Often Doesn't Answer

When you offer something real, it's natural to expect a response.

Not applause.
Not agreement.
Just a sign that what you shared was received.

But most of the time, the world doesn't answer — not because it didn't hear you, but because it doesn't know how to meet you.

We live in environments that are optimized for reaction, not reflection. Fast signals. Simple emotions. Clear sides. Your honesty doesn't fit easily into those systems. It doesn't give people a quick role to play.

So they hesitate.

They scroll past.
They change the subject.
They look, but don't touch.

This is especially true when what you offer carries depth. Depth asks something of the person encountering it. It asks them to feel, to notice themselves, to be present. Many people are not prepared for that, even if they want to be.

So instead of responding, they withdraw.

Silence, in this sense, is not absence.

It is **avoidance**.

People don't avoid what is meaningless.
They avoid what might move them.

That's why the quiet after you speak can feel so personal and yet be so impersonal at the same time. Your nervous system experiences it as rejection, but psychologically, it's more often a retreat.

The world is not organized to hold sincerity. It's organized to circulate signals. When you send something that isn't designed for circulation, it doesn't always come back with a reply.

That doesn't make what you shared less real.

It means you spoke into a space that wasn't built for listening.

This is where many people decide to harden, to perform, or to disappear.

**Hold On** is about choosing something else:

Staying present with the truth of what you offered,
even when the world stays quiet.

**EYE OF THE STORM**

You don't have to take the silence personally.

You don't have to fill it.
You don't have to make it mean something about you.

You spoke.
That was real.

Whether anyone answered or not
doesn't change that.

The space after you speak
is not empty.

It is just quiet.

And you are still here inside it.

Hold.

# Chapter 6 — Dismissal, Mockery, and the Laughing Emoji

### How People Deflect When They Don't Want to Feel

Most mockery is not cruelty.

It is **self-protection**.

When someone encounters something sincere, something vulnerable, or something that touches a part of themselves they've been avoiding, their nervous system feels a surge of sensation. Not necessarily pain — just **contact**.

Contact is uncomfortable when you haven't practiced it.

So instead of staying with the feeling, people reach for something that pushes it away.

A joke.
A scoff.
A laughing emoji.
A sarcastic comment.

These are not expressions of superiority. They are **deflections**.

Mockery creates distance. It lets someone feel in control again when something inside them was stirred. It says, "I don't have to take this seriously," even if, for a moment, they did.

That's why dismissive reactions often arrive without explanation. There's no real critique, no thoughtful disagreement — just a quick gesture that says, *I'm out.*

Not because what you offered was trivial.

But because it wasn't.

Depth doesn't invite everyone.
It exposes some people.

And when exposure feels unsafe, the easiest way out is to laugh.

So when someone meets your sincerity with dismissal, what you are seeing is not your failure to be worthy.

You are seeing their unwillingness to stay present with what you evoked.

That hurts.
But it's also strangely impersonal.

It's the sound of a door closing — not on you, but on a feeling they didn't want to have.

## Why Mockery Is Safer Than Contact

Contact requires something of you.

It asks you to feel what you're feeling.
It asks you to be present with what something stirred.
It asks you to stay.

Mockery asks for none of that.

Mockery is quick.
It's light.
It creates distance in a single gesture.

That's why it's so often used when something meaningful appears.

To actually meet something sincere, a person would have to slow down. They would have to notice their own reaction. They might even have to admit that something in them was touched.

That's vulnerable.

So instead, they laugh.

Not because it's funny —
but because it lets them leave without explaining why.

A laughing emoji is a tiny escape hatch. It says, "I don't have to engage," without having to say, "This affected me."

And because it's small and ambiguous, it carries no risk. No one can call you out for a laugh. It doesn't reveal what you felt. It doesn't require you to stand anywhere.

It just ends the moment.

That's why mockery can feel so cutting even when it's subtle. It doesn't attack your words. It erases the space where connection could have happened.

When you are offering something real, what you are really offering is a chance to be met.

Mockery declines that invitation.

Not loudly.
Not honestly.
Just quietly.

And that quiet refusal can sting more than open disagreement.

This is one of the hardest places to hold on — not because you were rejected, but because you were never really engaged with at all.

## EYE OF THE STORM

You don't have to carry what they threw back.

You don't have to chase after a door that closed.

What you offered was real.
What they did was a way of leaving.

Those two things are not the same.

Let the laughter fade.
Let the moment pass.

You are still here,
and nothing true about you was taken.

Trent Goodbaudy

## Chapter 7 — Being Seen and Not Met

### The Specific Pain of Exposure Without Response

There is a pain that doesn't come from being attacked.

It comes from being **visible and alone at the same time**.

You let yourself be seen. You put something honest into the light. And then — nothing reaches back.

No acknowledgment.
No resonance.
No sense that anyone is really there.

That kind of silence hits differently than rejection. Rejection says, *I see you and I don't want you.* Silence says, *I don't know what to do with what you showed me.*

And for a nervous system that just made itself visible, that feels like falling through space.

Exposure without response leaves you suspended. You don't know if you were understood. You don't know if you were accepted. You don't even know if you were noticed.

All you know is that you're out there now.

That's why this kind of pain can feel so raw. You didn't just lose approval. You lost orientation.

When we are met, we locate ourselves through the other. We feel our edges. We feel our presence. We know where we stand. But when there is no response, the space around us goes blank.

And blank space is terrifying to a social nervous system.

So you start filling it with questions:

Did I say too much?
Did I misread something?
Was I foolish to care?

Those questions aren't self-criticism. They're attempts to find ground again.

The ache you feel when you're seen and not met is not weakness.

It's the sound of connection reaching out and finding nothing to touch.

That's one of the hardest places to hold on.

**Why This Hurts More Than Rejection**

Rejection, painful as it is, gives you a shape to stand against.

Someone says no.
Someone disagrees.
Someone pulls away.

There is a boundary there.
There is a form.

But when you are seen and not met, there is nothing solid to lean on.

No answer.
No edge.
No clear signal of what just happened.

Your nervous system stays open, waiting for a response that never arrives. And in that waiting, the pain keeps renewing itself.

This is why silence can feel so much worse than criticism.

Criticism lets you orient.
Silence leaves you floating.

You don't know whether to grieve, to defend yourself, to apologize, or to move on. You just feel exposed in an unfinished moment.

That unfinished quality is what makes it hurt so deeply.

It's not just that you weren't chosen.
It's that the connection you reached for was never completed.

And because humans are wired for relationship, an incomplete connection feels like a rupture, even if no one meant harm.

Understanding this doesn't make it stop hurting.

But it can keep you from turning that hurt into a story about your worth.

You weren't ignored because you were unimportant.

You were left unanswered because something didn't know how to meet what you brought.

Holding on here means not closing yourself in response to an open ending.

It means staying present even when the connection didn't form.

## Chapter 8 — Why Sincerity Feels Dangerous to Others

**What Your Honesty Activates in People**

Sincerity does something that most social interaction does not.

It brings people into contact with themselves.

When you speak honestly, when you show up without performance or armor, you don't just reveal who you are. You create a field where others feel what they are.

That can be unsettling.

Someone might suddenly notice their own guardedness.
Their own exhaustion.
Their own longing to be real.

And those feelings don't always feel safe.

So instead of moving toward what you offered, they pull back.

Not because your honesty was too much,
but because it made something inside them visible.

This is why sincere people are often described as "intense," "awkward," or "too much." Not because they are overwhelming, but because they reduce the distance that normally keeps everyone comfortable.

Most social systems are built on a certain amount of mutual pretending. We smooth things out. We keep things light. We avoid the deeper currents unless we're sure they'll be welcomed.

Sincerity disrupts that.

It asks, without asking, "Are you here too?"

And not everyone is ready to answer.

So when your honesty meets hesitation, withdrawal, or discomfort, it's not because you did something wrong.

It's because you touched something real.

## Why They Back Away Instead of Coming Closer

Coming closer requires risk.

To meet sincerity with sincerity, a person would have to open themselves. They would have to step out of the role they're playing and into the uncertainty of being seen.

That's not something most people have been taught how to do.

So when honesty appears, instead of moving toward it, they retreat to what feels familiar: politeness, distance, humor, distraction, silence.

Those are not signs of indifference.

They are signs of fear.

Fear of being exposed.
Fear of saying the wrong thing.
Fear of not knowing who they are without their mask.

Backing away is how people protect the structures they live inside.

And because of that, sincere people often feel lonely even in rooms full of others. They are present in a way the environment is not designed to hold.

Understanding this doesn't remove the ache.

But it does make one thing clear:

When you are not met, it is not because you lacked something.

It is because you offered something many people don't know how to receive.

**EYE OF THE STORM**

You don't have to make yourself smaller to be safe.

You don't have to dim what is real in you.

If something backed away,
it was because you stood where feeling lives.

That place is not wrong.

You are allowed to be here,
just as you are,
even when others cannot come with you.

Hold.

# PART III — WHEN YOU STAY

Trent Goodbaudy

## Chapter 9 — What It Means to Remain

**The Difference Between Staying and Freezing**

From the outside, staying and freezing can look the same.

Both are still.
Both don't run.
Both don't react.

But inside, they are completely different.

Freezing happens when your system is overwhelmed. It shuts down to survive. You stop feeling. You go numb. You disconnect from what's happening because it's too much to stay present with.

Staying is the opposite.

Staying is when you feel everything and don't disappear.

It is not passive.
It is not resignation.
It is not giving up.

It is **contact in motion**.

When you stay, you are aware of the fear, the grief, the uncertainty — and you are still here inside it. You don't collapse into it, and you don't run from it. You let it move through you while you remain present.

Freezing makes time feel thick and stuck.
Staying makes time feel alive, even when it's hard.

One disconnects you from yourself.
The other keeps you connected.

That's why staying takes more strength than leaving. It requires you to keep your heart open in a place where it would be easier to close.

This is what **Hold On** is really pointing to.

Not gripping something that's gone.
Not forcing something to be what it was.

Just remaining in contact with what is,
even when it hurts.

That is not weakness.

That is presence.

## How Presence Outlasts Chaos

Chaos is loud.

It pulls at your attention.
It fills your mind with urgency.
It makes everything feel unstable and temporary.

Presence is quiet.

It doesn't argue with what's happening.
It doesn't try to control the waves.
It simply stays where you are.

That's why presence lasts longer than chaos.

Chaos needs energy to keep going — fear, reaction, resistance. Presence does not. It draws from something deeper: the simple fact that you are here, breathing, sensing, aware.

When you stay present, the storm can rage without carrying you away. You feel the movement, but you are not defined by it. You experience the uncertainty, but you are not erased by it.

This doesn't make life easy.

It makes it **real**.

The storms pass.
The waves change.
What remains is the one who stayed.

And that is what this book is quietly teaching you how to be.

Not unshakable.
Not immune.

Just here,
long enough for the world to move around you.

# Chapter 10 — Holding Without Hardening

## Why Becoming Tough Costs You Contact

When something hurts long enough, toughness starts to look like relief.

You stop expecting.
You stop reaching.
You stop letting things touch you.

From the outside, this can look like strength. You don't flinch anymore. You don't hope. You don't get disappointed.

But what you've really done is trade pain for **distance**.

Hardening is not resilience.
It is **withdrawal**.

You're still here physically, but emotionally you've stepped back. You don't feel as much — not because things have gotten better, but because you've closed the channels that let feeling in.

That costs you something.

Contact with others.
Contact with yourself.
Contact with what's alive.

You might feel safer, but you also feel flatter. Quieter. Less moved. And over time, that quiet can start to feel like loneliness, even if you're surrounded by people.

This is the danger of becoming tough.

It protects you from being hurt again, but it also protects you from being touched again.

**Hold On** is not about building armor that keeps everything out.

It's about learning how to stay open without being destroyed.

That's a different kind of strength — one that doesn't require you to disappear from your own life.

## How to Stay Open Without Collapsing

Staying open does not mean letting everything in.

It means letting what is real touch you
without letting it define you.

There is a middle place between armor and exposure — a place
where you feel what's happening, but you are not overwhelmed by it.
That place is built through **presence**, not protection.

When you stay present, you don't need to harden to survive. You
notice what hurts. You notice what moves. You breathe. You feel
your body. You stay here.

That simple act keeps you intact.

Collapsing happens when you lose yourself inside what you feel.
Hardening happens when you push feeling away. Presence lets
feeling move through you without either extreme.

This is not something you force.

It grows as you learn to trust that you can feel and still be okay.

Every time you stay with a sensation instead of fleeing it, you build
this capacity. Every time you let something move through you
without turning into a story about who you are, you strengthen it.

This is what real resilience looks like.

Not indifference.
Not numbness.

Just the quiet ability to remain open
in a moving world.

**EYE OF THE STORM**

You don't have to close to be safe.

You don't have to harden to survive.

What is real in you
is not fragile.

Let it breathe.
Let it feel.

You are still here,
and that is enough.

## Chapter 11 — The Quiet Strength Nobody Applauds

**Why Real Endurance Is Invisible**

Most of what we call strength is loud.

It shows itself in victories, in speeches, in visible perseverance. It has something to point to. Something that can be admired.

But the strength that keeps a person whole through a storm rarely looks like anything at all.

It looks like getting up when no one is watching.
Like continuing to care when nothing is returned.
Like staying present in a life that doesn't offer reassurance.

There is no audience for that.

No metric.
No applause.

And because it leaves no obvious mark, people often mistake it for nothing.

But this is the kind of strength that actually carries you forward.

It doesn't break records.
It doesn't make headlines.
It just quietly refuses to disappear.

Every time you choose not to numb.
Every time you don't harden.
Every time you stay with what is real even when it's lonely —

That is endurance.

And it is happening inside you whether anyone sees it or not.

The world is very good at noticing what performs.

It is not very good at noticing what remains.

But what remains is what lasts.

**How to Live Without Needing to Be Seen**

There is a deep freedom in no longer needing proof that you are here.

When you stop waiting for recognition, something inside you relaxes. You don't disappear — you become steadier. Your actions no longer depend on whether anyone is watching. They come from what feels true instead of what might be rewarded.

This doesn't make you invisible.

It makes you **rooted**.

You still feel the longing to be met. You still care. But you don't collapse when the response doesn't come. You don't have to turn yourself into something louder just to be acknowledged.

Living without needing to be seen is not about withdrawing from the world.

It's about not outsourcing your sense of being real.

You know when you're here.
You know when you're honest.
You know when you stayed.

That's enough.

And from that place, whatever recognition does arrive can be received — not as proof of worth, but as a simple human exchange.

This is one of the quietest forms of strength there is.

And it is one of the most durable.

Trent Goodbaudy

# Chapter 12 — Staying When Everything Moves

**What Holding On Actually Looks Like in Daily Life**

Holding on is not a dramatic act.

It doesn't look like white-knuckled effort or heroic endurance. Most days, it looks almost ordinary.

You wake up.
You breathe.
You notice how you feel.
You choose not to disappear from it.

Holding on means you keep your body where it is, even when your mind wants to escape into stories, distractions, or self-criticism. It means you feel the ache in your chest instead of rushing past it. You let the uncertainty be there without forcing it to resolve.

In daily life, this might look like:

Pausing before you react.
Staying with a conversation even when it feels awkward.
Letting yourself feel disappointed without turning it into a judgment about who you are.

These are small moments, but they are where presence lives.

You don't need to be perfect at them.

Every time you notice that you're here — sensing, breathing, feeling — you are already holding on.

The storm doesn't always come as a big wave.

Sometimes it comes as a long, quiet stretch where nothing is clear.

And this is where holding on becomes something you practice, not something you achieve.

Not by gripping the world.

But by staying inside yourself as it moves.

## How to Keep Contact When the World Keeps Shifting

The world will not stop changing for you.

People will move.
Projects will evolve.
Meanings will rise and fall.

What you can keep is **contact**.

Contact with your breath.
Contact with your sensations.
Contact with what feels true in this moment.

When you keep that, the shifting world does not take you with it.

You can feel sadness without becoming sad.
You can feel uncertainty without becoming lost.
You can feel the ground move without falling.

This is not detachment.

It is presence with a spine.

You don't float above your life.
You stand inside it.

And when you do, even the storm becomes something you can be with rather than something that sweeps you away.

That is what **Hold On** has been pointing to from the beginning.

Not a future where nothing moves.

But a way of being here
no matter how much it does.

## Closing — You're Still Here

Nothing in this book was meant to take you somewhere else.

It was meant to keep you here.

You may not feel different in any dramatic way.
You may not feel solved, healed, or complete.

What you might feel is something quieter:

A little more present.
A little more in your body.
A little less afraid of what moves.

That's enough.

Storms don't end because you understand them.
They end because they move through.

So do the feelings you've met in these pages.
So do the questions.
So do the moments of doubt, the ache of not being met, the quiet grief of something slipping.

You didn't have to fix any of it.

You stayed.

That staying is not a small thing.

It means you didn't harden when it hurt.
It means you didn't disappear when it got quiet.
It means you didn't turn yourself into something else just to feel safe.

You remained in contact with what was real.

That is what keeps a person whole.

There will be other waves after this.
Other silences.
Other moments when you offer something honest and don't know what will come back.

When they arrive, you don't need to remember every word you read here.

Just remember this:

You can feel.
You can breathe.
You can stay.

And that means you are still here.

Nothing more is required.

## EYE OF THE STORM

Nothing needs to be added now.

Nothing needs to be taken away.

You are here.
You have been here.
You are still here.

Let the sea move.
Let the sky change.

You remain.

## About the Author

Trent Goodbaudy writes about what it means to remain human in a world that is always moving. His work is not built around formulas, optimization, or performance. It is built around something quieter: the ability to stay present when certainty disappears and when the world doesn't always answer back.

The ideas in *Hold On* did not come from theory. They emerged from lived experience — from offering something sincere into the world and meeting the strange combination of silence, misunderstanding, and quiet resistance that often follows when something real is shared. That space, where effort is given and nothing obvious returns, became the soil this book grew out of.

Rather than turning that experience into bitterness or bravado, Trent chose to listen to it. He followed what it revealed about the nervous system, about contact, and about the difference between being seen and being met. Over time, those reflections formed the gentle, steady voice you find in these pages — a voice that doesn't demand, persuade, or perform, but stays.

*Hold On* is part of the LibertyTruth series, a growing body of work dedicated to clarity, discernment, and inner stability in an increasingly loud and reactive world. Each book in the series explores a different facet of what it means to live without surrendering yourself to noise, pressure, or false certainty.

Trent lives and works in the American West, where wide skies and long distances make it easier to remember that not everything meaningful happens where people are looking. He continues to write, build, and publish from that place — not to be louder, but to remain present.

This book exists because sometimes the most important thing a person can do is not to prove anything, not to win, and not to be understood...

…but simply to stay.

## About LibertyTruth

LibertyTruth.org exists for readers who are finished with slogans, certainty theater, and answers that arrive prepackaged.

The books and materials published through LibertyTruth are not designed to persuade, recruit, or motivate. They are designed to clarify—to make visible the patterns that quietly shape belief, behavior, and consent in everyday life.

The goal is simpler—and harder.

To help you see what you may already be living inside, so that whatever choices follow are genuinely your own.

Visit **LibertyTruth.org** if you want to continue exploring this work—quietly, independently, and without instruction.

Made in the USA
Coppell, TX
22 February 2026

72089121R00049